Who was David Gould?

compiled by

Joan (Angel, Deirdre, Tracey ...) Gould

David Gould is identified as the illustrator of this book and Joan Gould as its author in accordance with Section 77 of the Copyright, Designs and Patent Act, 1988.

ISBN: 978-1-7384493-4-7

Privately published by the author for a limited circulation of 150 copies
© Joan Gould 2024
High Croft
South Woodchester
Gl5 5EP

The text is set in Monotype Plantin, released in 1913 for hot-metal typesetting and becoming a digital font in 2001.

Printed by Printed Word Publishing, Part of Scantech Lithographic Ltd.

Design: Jane Dorner
Endpapers: Willow Boughs William Morris wallpaper © Sanderson Design Group

Who was David Gould?

Angel and David – and their many alter egos – are the
main characters in this story.

Contents

Angel and David sold their house in London at a time when other houses were not selling at all.

Glad to get shot o' this old heap of bricks

And we shalln't have to decorate the big sitting-room OR worry about the potential and ever-present subsidence

FOR SOLD
this DESIRABLE RESIDENCE WITH ALL FAULTS
SALUBRIOUS 'OMES INC AGENTS

FOR SALE
FOR SALE
FOR SALE
FOR SALE

Gloucestershire 'ide out... Oh yus...

Two miles to Lypiatt Two 'n'arf to Gatcombe Park an' almost six to 'igh Grove me dear...

Quaite convenient for the Kents, the Phillipses and the Waleses — Royal South Glos, eh

Introduction

When my husband David died in 2004 I asked friends if I could scan copies of illustrated letters they had received from him over the years. I also found lots of the illustrations I had as valentines, birthday cards and funny little notes. I knew then that I wanted to make a book of his wonderful caricatures, but it has taken until now to be able to do it.

The skill of caricature lies in the way it captures the essence of the person. Friends and family all knew the people and thought the drawings hilarious and clever; not knowing the people takes away some of the charm and fun and, because of that, I have selected drawings which seemed to me to stand up in their own right as 'just funny'. A lot of the illustrations are from letters, so not all our friends and family appear here, either because in the years covered there was no correspondence between us or things simply got lost. I haven't attempted to identify all the people because who they are will not matter to strangers and those of us illustrated will all know who we are!

David had lived in London all his life, but knew Gloucestershire well and we had several very good friends there, so when we could move to the country that was the obvious place to go. My being made redundant from Edward Arnold enabled me to work freelance from home. David had been semi-retired for some years after working as a picture restorer and 'art expert', latterly with Sotheby's as their Victorian picture expert. He had a brief exposure to fame when he unearthed the fraud of Samuel Palmer drawings and paintings produced by Tom Keating and from being in the early episodes of The Antiques Road Show. We moved to High Croft in the summer of 1989.

David adapted instantly to the life of a country, squire as so many of his drawings show, particularly those of Lord Molesworth and his butler – parts convincingly played by David. Thinking back I wondered where Lord Molesworth came from and am sure it was a development of the Molesworth in *Down with School* who transmogrified into Lord M. I was rather dismayed to find a newspaper cutting which mentioned a real Lord Molesworth, but he died in 1725.

David had time to amass a huge library (and the space to house it!) and books remained one of his great passions. He would produce funny little drawings at the drop of a hat, although he took care and trouble over them. It is noticeable, that he remained almost ageless in the drawings, but in so many ways that is just how he was too. He slowed down over the years of course but always bounced back at the mention of a 'little tootle' in the car, particularly if it involved a visit to a bookshop or a bookfair!

He had done funny drawings all his life and in our time together I saw how he would just pick on one or two features of a person and that became 'them' ever afterwards. Little Deirdre (my second name is Deirdre) had blue hands; Ursula, a friend, always wore a little hat; my father had bandy legs. At High Croft we had a battery of imaginary staff, who one could blame if the washing-up had not been done, the cooking spoilt or you couldn't find something – clearly someone had hidden it! Wayne and Tracey, the domestics, came from London with little Deirdre, the Lerts, (B A Lert and Company did gardening).

David Gould – my Lord Molesworth – and his world will now continue to live on in the letters and drawings scattered around friends and family as well as in this book.

Angel Gould
High Croft 2024

High Croft – the Staff

We needed 'staff' at High Croft, but only had imaginary ones, ourselves of course! Here are the butler and little Deirdre, the office boy and Sylvia the milkmaid. In our London house we had Wayne and Tracey, who joined us sometimes. They always felt put upon.

The RULES for MILKMAIDS

1 Deliver the milk
2 Gossip

If the rules are reversed the milk is overlooked.

Sh(r)ove orf Tuesday
19 Feb 1980

Dere Madum

Its orl a
BIT
TO
MUTCH

16 July 80

The Browns were just across the valley and knew all about our imaginary staff.

There was plenty of leisure for reading and reflecting, puzzling over the daily crossword, consulting reference books for clues, and the joy of having solved the day's task.

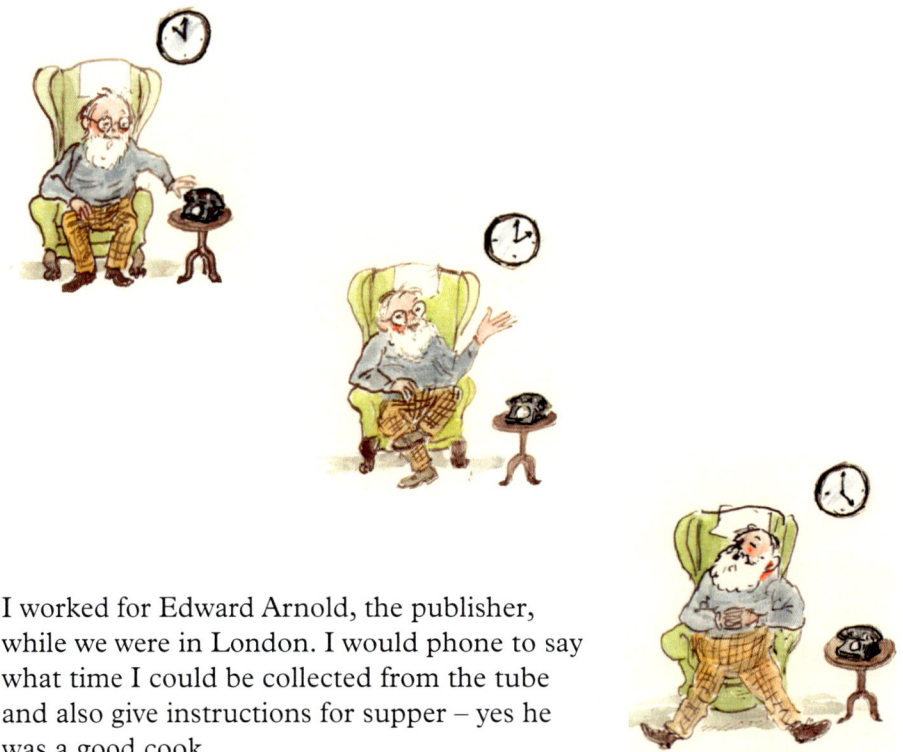

I'VE DONE IT!
I'VE DONE IT!!

I worked for Edward Arnold, the publisher, while we were in London. I would phone to say what time I could be collected from the tube and also give instructions for supper – yes he was a good cook.

Lord Molesworth, having not enough to do
Reads the daily papers through and through
Times, Telegraph, and Daily Worker, too
    Ennui is so boring, don'tcherknow!

His well-stock'd mind with indignation true
Induces him to pen a line or two -
On things from kitchenware to Timbuctoo.
    Ennui is so boring, don'tcherknow!

The Field and Country Life engage his wits,
'Outrag'd of Woodchester" he signs his bits,
Sending the Editors into purple fits!
    Ennui is so boring, don'tcherknow!

Doesn't everybody have a pedigree?

From time to time David was asked to autheticate a picture. He was an authority on the Victorian period. Authenticating a picture as being by the artist in question, of course, had tremendous influence on the sale value and so such expertise was itself highly valued.

5

Books

David's great passion was for books, especially in later life when we even converted a double-garage into 'The Bookroom'. He had an immmense library and loved, as I still do, wandering along the shelves, selecting something that caught his eye and settling down to read it. Visitors often commented on the number of books and I did try and control the flow somewhat. Thank goodness he never worked out the internet and Amazon!

I collected little books – for obvious reasons. Books are very heavy and of course they were mostly hardback, and often large paper editions – another love.

Books were always important, even from an early age as the drawing of himself as a very young man shows. This childhood bookplate maybe suggests 'collecting' was already developing! And yes, he did read them all, not from cover to cover as there were clearly too many for that, but he knew what was inside everything he bought and when he got a new book would settle down and, as he said, 'rip the guts' out of it – or them as was more usually the case!

Self reading. Gould 1940

COR-delishus oh dave?!

NOT SO DRY AS DUST, What!

Redit Redit Redit

Visits to bookshops were often the focus for a 'little tootle' but then there were the bookfairs! We never left a shop or bookfair without something. We had the space, but in the end it was more than filled of course. Books are promiscuous and breed very fast when left to their own devices on shelves.

One of his greatest friends was Ian Hodgkins a bookseller, who lived with another Ian, little Ian, at Slad. David and he used to leaf through catalogues, discussing the merits of particular editions – large paper was a particular fancy to them both. He also went book-hunting with another bibliophile, Nicky Mander.

Lizie, the recipient of this letter, is one of our oldest and dearest friends and she received more notes and letters than anyone.

Home Improvements

Decorating, sometimes with help, involved
fixing things that didn't work and, of course,
building bookcases. David was a very
competent craftsman and made all our many

shall I help measure 'em?

Really can't think what went wrong...

I've got some NEW cable and NEW plugs.
We are going to rewire these lamps, each
with half the wire, and we are fitting
NEW plugs. I'll do one and you
do the other...

15 March 92

Got mine done first

TIMBER

Gardening

Gardening was more Lady Molesworth's preserve – well almost exclusively, although David sometimes came to 'supervise'! The garden wasn't the only thing that changed over the years.

Greetings
from
A couple of rakes

GROWMORE
OR LESS

In the early days we grew all our own vegetables, and even gave pots of chicory as Christmas presents. Here are a couple of our labels.

The garden had the typical Victorian box hedges which all needed clipping of course. Fortunately they were just waist height, but did lend themselves to thoughts of topiary. The two topiarists had recently been on a course and took the project in hand.

The garden was a bit of a challenge to start, but I soon got skilled garden terrorists to do the jobs requiring much skill.

DIS COB BEL LUS

SLU TWI THA DISH

Help

DISTINCTIVE TOPIARY
15 ELSIE R^D
East Dulwich
LONDON SE22

26^p

15

Going Abroad

EN NORMANDIE et BRETAGNE

Angel us JFM

Then there were the holidays 'abroad' in France and Italy. Compiling the journal was an essential part of the holiday, sitting quietly in the evening, drawing, chatting and enjoying the odd glass of local vintage.

Typical Angelbeck organising her man

The caption to the top illustration reads:

> *Angel:* And having got you this far along the plage, you are jolly well going to enjoy yourself.
> *David:* There's sand in my sandwich.
> *Angel:* That's only because I dropped it.

So we went to look at rock pools. Sometimes he read while I soaked up the sun – far too much obviously. Some days it rained and rained.

We were fascinated by an old man who came into the bar every morning as we had breakfast. He drank his single glass of red wine in a single gulp and left.

Deirdre who came too, on condition that she helped carry the picnic – or so they said – quickly decided to adopt a French style and renamed herself . . .

. . . Arsinoë.

de petite taille et de grande taille ....

Monday 13th June 1988

BLEU DE TRAVAIL

DÉMODÉ

fait sur mesure

Acheter quelque chose en prêt-à-porter !

We sometimes went on holiday with friends: booksellers Big Ian and Little Ian and Jacquie. We all tried to get David into *bleu de travail*, but believe it or not, couldn't find quite the right shape or size.

19

The Joy of Pets

Barbara and Mary, the Dollies, wanted a dog – for a while. They already had two cats.

Darling Dollies – I said to Angel "How COULD you leave those two innocents at a bus-stop at the Oval !!!"

GENTS

13.XI.99

Fetch, Mary...

14.XI.9

Well I never!! DID SHE?

WOZZAT???

Hoots mon - ye nivuer can tell

FAGS

Jolly good luck to 'em, I say

Your turn to scooper poop

Your turn to scooper poop

12 Nov 1999

Visiting Friends

Judith and Simon Verity lived in Wiltshire and were not long married when we first stayed with them. Children arrived, Polly, Tom and John and David did little drawings for them. The pigloo was part of such a story booklet. Simon is a sculptor and letterer and Judith also does lettering and wonderful linocuts. David and I did our first printing on their little Albion. Judith in later years, when Simon was in America, kept the workshop going with, amongst other jobs, beautifully lettered gravestones. They lived a very spartan life which was full of laughter and jokes– or jolly japes as I'm sure we'd have called them then.

To

The ELMS Farmhouse
UPPER MINETY
WILTSHIRE Malmesbury SN16 9PR

SIMPLE SIMON
SIMPLE SOUL
BOUGHT A BOOK
ON BIRTH CONTROL
JVDGING BY OVR JVDE'S CONDITION
IT MVST HAVE BEEN AN OLD EDN.

Marie Stope's House BALHAM

Matron: J. Angelbeck

TO
DANCE
IS TO
LIVE

PIGLOO

Welcome

JUDITH...
COME HERE...
I DON'T
THINK THIS
PLUMBLINE
IS STRAIGHT

PSALM
127
v.1

VERITY
HALL

MCM
LXXIV
AD

PURBeck

NORMAN
JEWSON
Consultant
Archt

POLLY

ROSALIND

TOM

THIS
STEWN
WAS
LAID

BY
JUDITH

SIM
ON

The text of the letter said: 'It wasn't bad, it wasn't bad, the little bit of pie we had. Larks and oysters were not present, nor any scrap of local pheasant, and yet, and yet, what Judith cook'd, tasted superbly, and it look'd *superb*. Our hearts began to beat as we sat down and 'gan to eat.'

Monday
23 February '81

01·874 2620   Thursday 31st January 1974
                evening

Dear Printers & Linocutters, Cooks, Gardeners, Stonecutters, Letterers & Washing-uppers & Tom minders & Polly protectors & Rosalyn'd milkers & the birds that sing in the garden — Greetings. There is always a jolly scramble for the early morning letters which scatter on the floor.

But this morning things were different: all was dignity. The Postman rang the bell and handed me a parcel inscribed

DAVID GOULD R.A.

And what a parcel!!

SCOTLAND YARD

Alert all booksellers

WANTED

for questioning

At present under the name
GEOFFREY BAILEY

formerly
Dyllan's righthand man

Illustrious con-man to the
Book Trade

I don't remember many fancy-dress parties, but there were many others. Geoffrey, a frequent visitor, had just lost his job at Hatchard's in London, which prompted these drawings, Judith was always drawn with an overlarge nose! She just laughed.

Owlpen Manor

"'scuse oi, zur, there be a small sharratong o' us from the Mumbleset Naturial 'istory and Handiquanian sosciety an' we be a wonderin', me Lord, if you or your missus do do teas ....."

NOT OPEN
EVERY LEAP
YEAR
Admission £5.

Darleenk – eesn't ees ship, the most loveliest of ships?

Well, ahem, Karen, it isn't PURE Cottswold y'know...

Baa who is this Reindeer anyway?

3 July 75. Just to say Thank you for calling today. As ever David

K ... "Wow! Niccy! Look at these!"
N ... "They sh'd onlie be gathered at y'e wane of y'e moone, with your lefte foote upon a toade and a bunch of muggeworte in y'e lefte hande, and a bunch of adders tongues in y'e righte hande, saying y'e paternoster six tymes ...."!

David had a van in the early days before we moved from London. It was just big enough to sleep in. We often camped along a particular 'green road' near Sapperton and even invited guests for dinner.

David just loved Owlpen, the Manders' home, and Nicky and Karin were always so hospitable.

25

A Trip to Bath

We stayed with Barley Roscoe when she lived in Bath setting up the new Craft Study Centre (now moved to Farnham). As we chatted around him David compiled a little diary of the weekend events, finishing and binding it later when we returned home. We had lots of energy then, particularly Barley who organised dinner parties – here with the Verities and Ann Heckle the calligrapher – and visits to concerts.

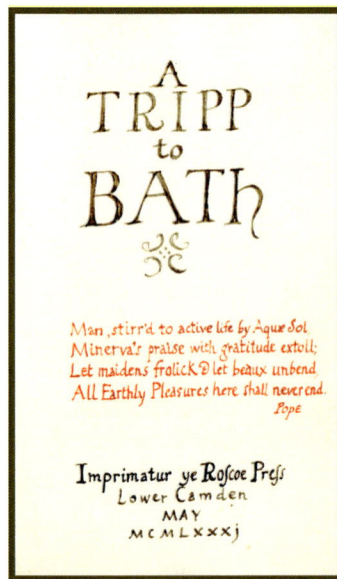

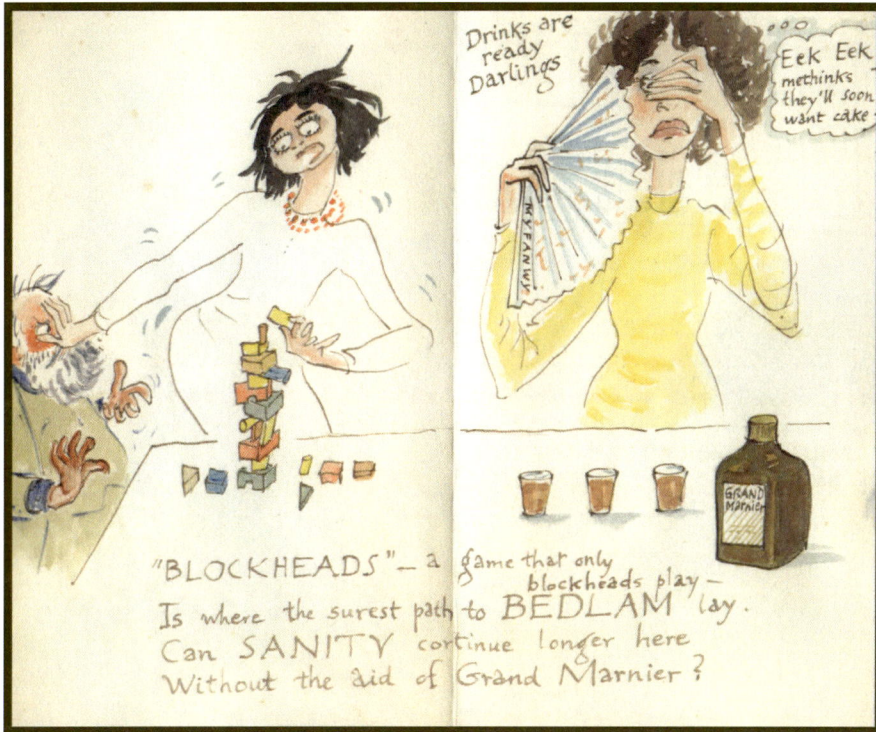

"BLOCKHEADS" — a game that only
blockheads play —
Is where the surest path to BEDLAM lay.
Can SANITY continue longer here
Without the aid of Grand Marnier?

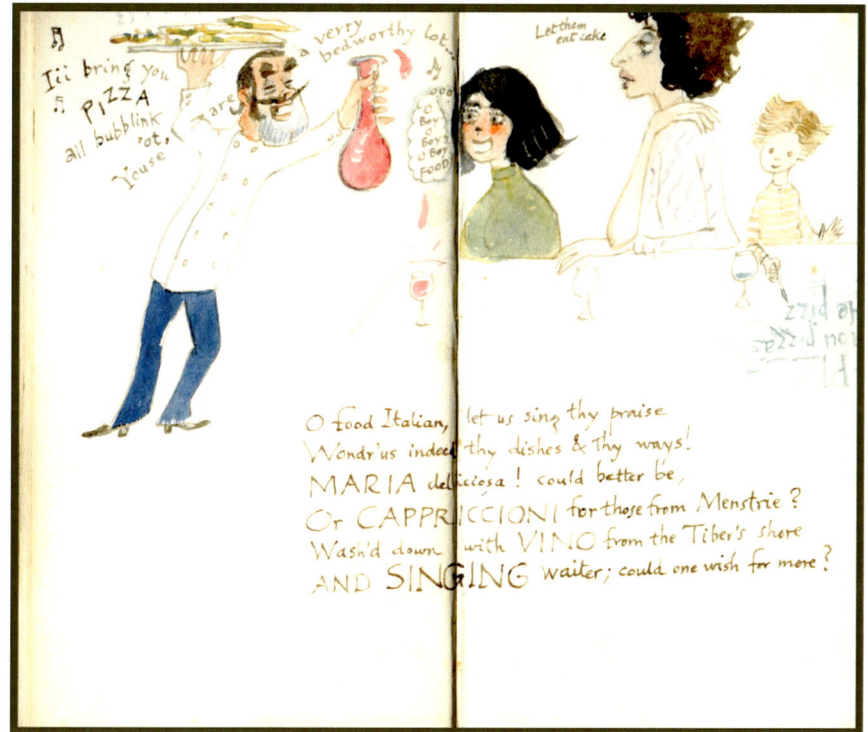

O food Italian, let us sing thy praise
Wondr'us indeed thy dishes & thy ways!
MARIA deliciosa ! could better be,
Or CAPPRICCIONI for those from Menstrie ?
Wash'd down with VINO from the Tiber's shore
AND SINGING waiter; could one wish for more ?

Monday

Breakfast is over and we must shed a tear,
MAY indeed has been too wet this year;
Our Holiday is done in Floods & rain
Thank you, dear Barley for having us again

A Little of What you Fancy ... is never quite enough

David was always 'portly', partly because he took no exercise and partly because he loved food and sitting around with friends over a meal in the evening, or lunch, or breakfast! He was a good, traditional cook and bought quantities of books about cooking and recipes – maybe in the faint hope I might try some. So he often sabotaged real efforts at diets. I tried endlessly to encourage diets and light exercise, all to no avail of course! Great play was made about how I grew larger as he faded away to a shadow.

Ee bah gum –
they're good
little eaters

Eat up –
more coming...

As from 14 June 1993

RULES of this FUCKIN 'OLE are as follows:

7 am — Gerrup

7.10 — Tea for the Master

8 sharp — Hearty breakfast
No cereals
only Porridge
Egg boiled + toast
or
Eggs & bacon -
Marmalade + toast
Coffee

12.30 on the dot
Scrummy lunch
by previous agreed discussion

4 — Tea, toast, honey, cake

6.30 Dinner. 3 courses
Soup (clear)
Fish/meat & 2 veg
Pudden.
Lady of the house can eat
when she fuckin' well pleases.

YOU ARE GOING TO WEIGHT WATCHERS

4th July 1988
INDEPENDENCE DAY
So what !

I won't go !
I won't go !
I won't go !
AND THAT'S THAT.

It's not really ME sitting here!

Nor ME !

VERY ODD some of the folk who come...

GRIM SOAKS

OR YOU

Take that off AT ONCE – it doesn't fit you anyway

25 Feb 85

He was eventually persuaded to try Weight Watchers – for two weeks!

Hospitals and Health

Oh no!

I'm going to

COUGH!

13 XI '79

Do they always come back from France like this?

YES, Doctor — But we soon knock 'em into shape..

ANTI FREEZE

There were periods of ill health and sometimes visits to the Royal Brompton Hospital in London where David had been a patient since 1951 with a chronic lung condition. Eventually this affected his heart, hence the suggestion of surgery – not actually possible it transpired. Needless to say David hated hospitals and was certainly even at home a 'difficult patient'!

Speech bubble: Oh NO!! Not back to Ottawa!!

IV bag labels: SHEEP DIP — MURRAYS MINTS — MAPLE SYRUP — DOLLY MIX — ST VALENTINE MIX

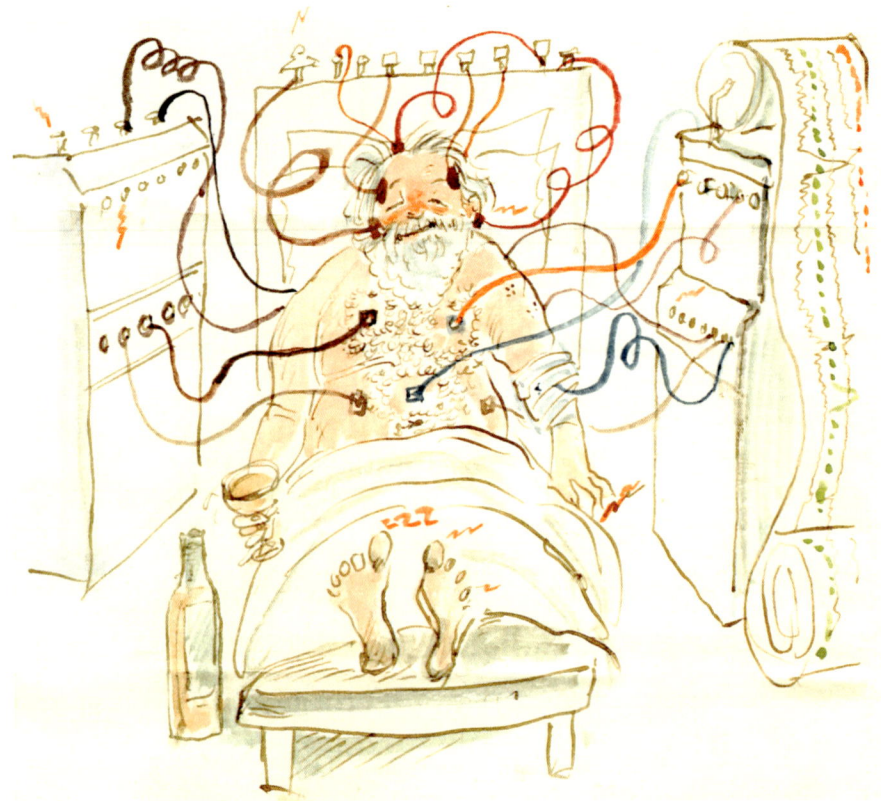

Male nurse and hospital orderly

Him: Do you like working in this hospital?
Her: Not 'arf, s'lovely 'ere. Can you tell me somfink?
Him: Yus, wot?
Her: Friend of mine's got flu. How long's it take?
Him: Confidentially, 'bout free months.

She wondered if he was under the weather — and she called-in the local medical man, who said:

"Without doubt, he has a heart condition. A small problem. I'll write a letter to The Royal Brompton Hospital. They will know what to do."

He was reluctant to go, so she pushed him.

The Surgeon and his staff were very pleased. "Soon sort you out," said the Professor. "Yum, yum," said the Nurse.

Give 'im the works, Nurse Nightingale!

The nurses did administer to his every want.

Dealing with Matron

David liked to pretend he was bossed around – well he needed it sometimes – and so 'matron' came into existence.

Dear Simon – I simply can't wait to get to Rodbourne ....

But...

Matron may come too ....

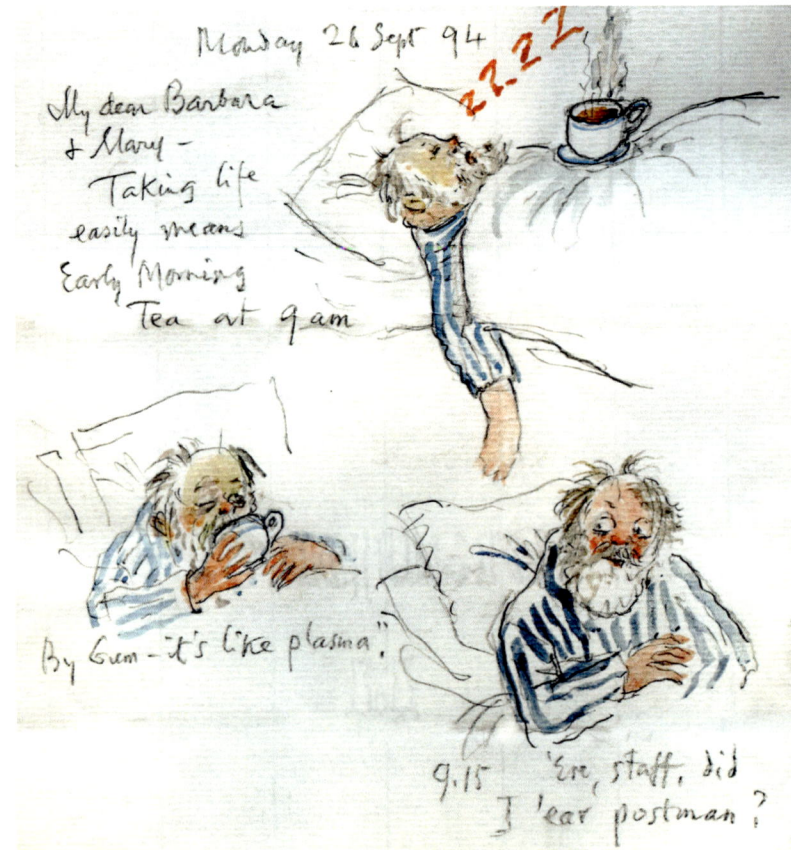

Monday 26 Sept 94

My dear Barbara & Mary –
Taking life easily means Early Morning Tea at 9am

By Gum – it's like plasma"

9.15 'Ere, staff, did I 'ear postman?

We can't go on meeting like this: someone will think you are unwell

Another View of Life

Early Taste and..   .. one week later.

9 Criffel Avenue
Streatham Hill
SW2 4AY

12th November 1986

Dearest old Draughtswoman (South 'ams Variety)

Has anybody seen Jacquie?

'ERCULE

Herewith one small and cuddly old Leotard avec 'ercule within, who now realises that his true metier has not as yet been fully exploited. He is now advertising his availability in the South Hams Art Sector, and anxiously awaits the call.

These are here just because they are funny, but the contexts are holidaying in the Dordogne with the Ians and Jacquie, who drew too. David became 'Ercule somewhere along the line. Sunbathing with Nicky Mander was totally ridiculous as they both avoided exposing a tiny bit of flesh to the sun!

35

Christmas Cards

David produced a Christmas card every year. At first these were lino cuts printed on our little Albion Model 4 printing press. Later we photocopied them to be tinted in water colour, but finally, wonder of wonders, we got a little colour printer. Interesting now to see how these cards refelect the speed of technolgical devlopment! Here are some of my favourites.

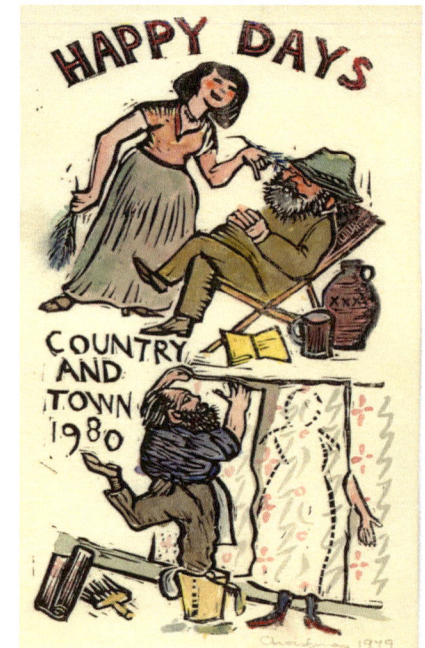

HAPPY DAYS

COUNTRY AND TOWN 1980

CHRISTMAS CHEER

Mush mush
-Helen n' Richard
-next

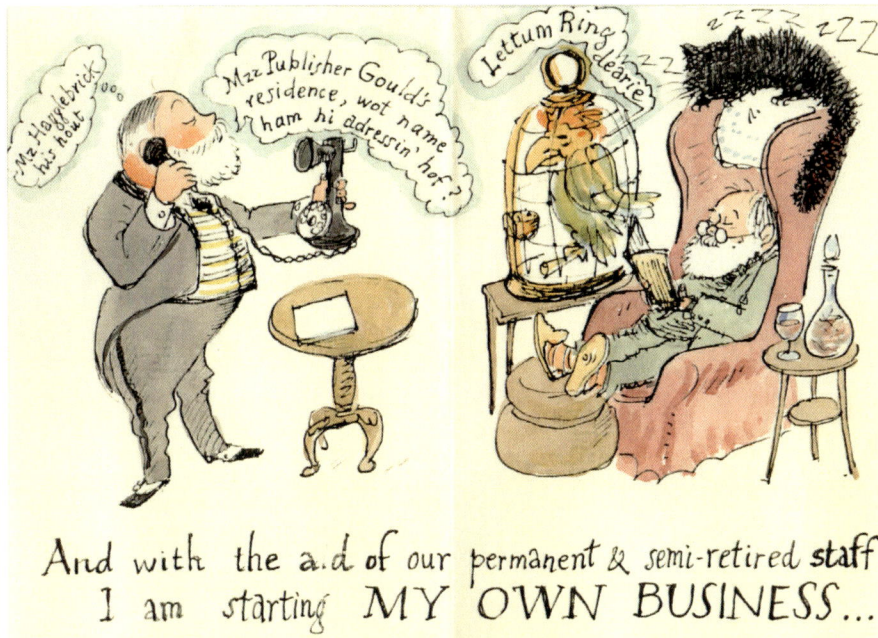

And with the a.d of our permanent & semi-retired staff I am starting MY OWN BUSINESS...

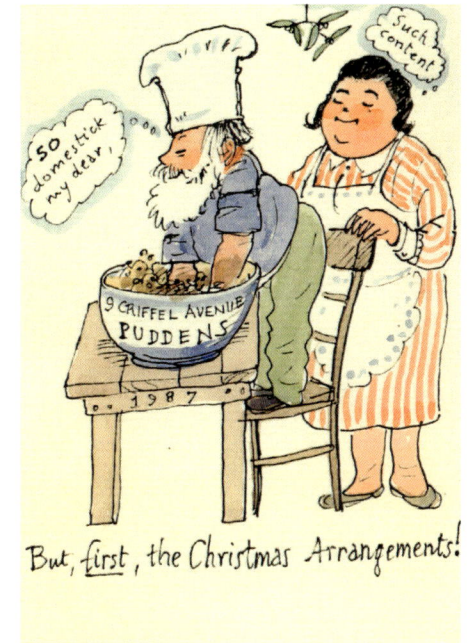

But, first, the Christmas Arrangements!

Happy Christmas 1986
from ANGEL and DAVID

LOVE to you ALL

Let 'em tint 'em themselves!

CRIFFEL CARDS for 1880's folk

What are you doing for OUR card?

I haven't a clue!

DONE IN ADVICE

NICE ONE DAVID

HAPPY CHRISTMAS

Warmest wishes from Angel 'n' David

Anagrams are the order of the day —
{ TIP MARSHY CHAPS
{ HAPPY CHRISTMAS

Your turn /

D·I·Y

Across :
1. Unknown quantity (not Y)
3. Best beer (for Roty)

Down
1. Triple Kisses } for Jude
2. Ditto .

Woodchester Court Never a
Cross Word Cards —
December 1997

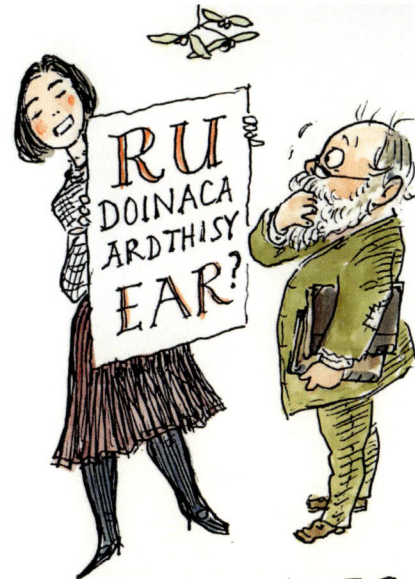

GREETINGS

CHRISTMAS CARD? did
you say? But who will do
it? Country life is very
exhausting, so, this year...

... we shall not go into
hibernation without making
an effort to produce a simple card to wish you a very
HAPPY CHRISTMAS

Warmest Greetings for Christmas
from Angel + David

Dec' 1993
South Woodchester
Play Group.

39

Happy Christmas
from
Angel & David Gould

HAPPY CHRISTMAS
Nevertheless

1994

From Angel and David Gould
High Croft (Woodchester Court)
South WOODCHESTER
Gloucestershire   GL5 5EP

'Taint bin too bad a-livin'
int' country,' as it lass?
O no, 'as such nice incon=
veniences, don't it . (verb sap)

CHRISTMAS
GREETINGS

from ANGEL
and DAVID

ARCADIAN
BLISS
from the
Woodchester Play Group

A
VERY
HAPPY
CHRISTMAS
19 99
ANGEL
and
DAVID

By Appointment

Wishing You
A Jolly Christmas from

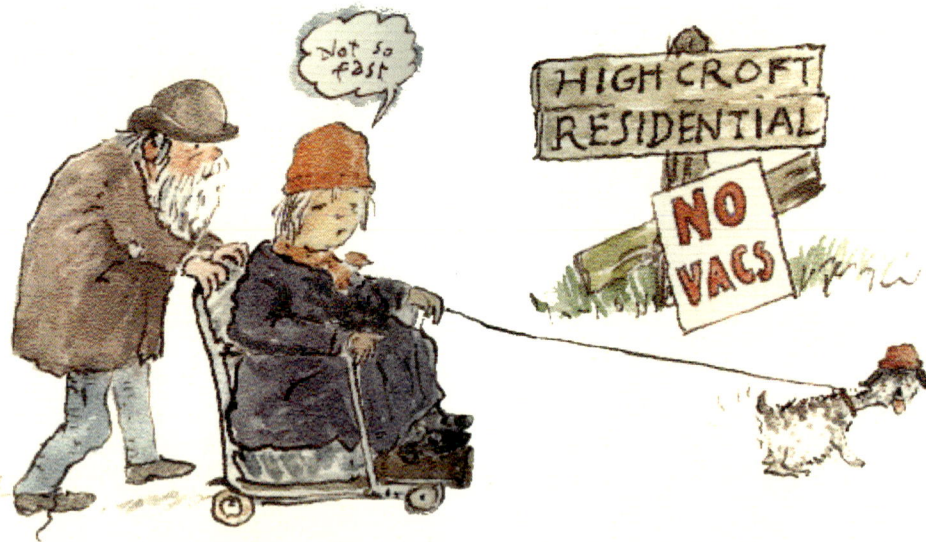

Not so
fast

David & Angel

HIGH CROFT
RESIDENTIAL

NO
VACS

CHRISTMAS
1
85

GREETINGS from
Angel & David [& Staff
P.T.O]

Now in hand

1880's Ales

XXXXX
XXXXX
XXXXX
XXXXX

Love from Wayne

Yore sincerly Tracey

9 Criffel Avenue is not a
Tea House

42

Thank you for sending us a card. So sorry our's is a bit late, but being postal services what they are I suppose we are lucky to have an occasional delivery & 'imself DID get round in 'is own sweet time

MERRY CHRISTMAS

It'll do for a New Year card IF I can get round to it!

To tint... or not to tint?

3 cheers f'r Ag!!

URGINT GEDDON WIV IT

SEASONS

GREETINGS

CHRISTMAS WISHES from ANGEL & DAVID

WE HAVE BUILT LOTS OF DRYSTONE WALLS IN THE GARDEN IDEAL FOR SUMMERTIME

1990

HIGH CROFT SANCTUARY SOUTH WOODCHESTER

Life at High Croft

The kitchen was the heart of the house in a way, partly because David used to sit at one end of the kitchen table as 'his area' where he did nearly all his drawings and because it was always warm with the Aga. Mrs Corps, who used to work for my mother and became an honorary granny and my father's cousin Harold, who used to be a pork butcher in Macclesfield, used to come and stay and we usually made marmalade then.

HAROLD'S DELIGHT
BY-GUM MARMALADE
1998

OLD HAT MARMALADE

16 January 1980

... while I would not for one moment criticise your otherwise admirable work, I must point out that you should not leave the bowl full of cold water and soaking greasy dishes: this is not to be recommended and must be avoided at all costs ...

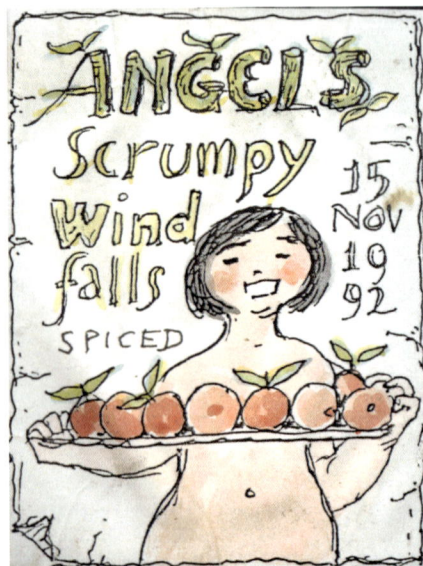

ANGEL'S Scrumpy Wind falls
SPICED
15 NOV 19 92

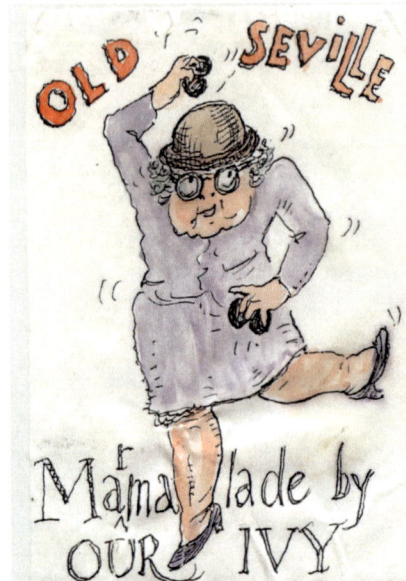

OLD SEVILLE
Marmalade by OUR IVY

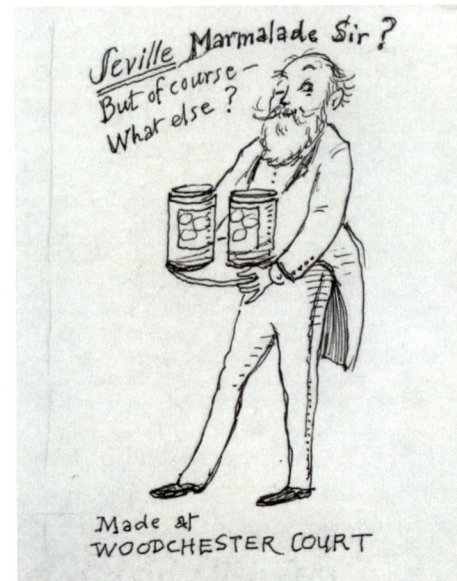

Seville Marmalade Sir?
But of course — What else?
Made at WOODCHESTER COURT

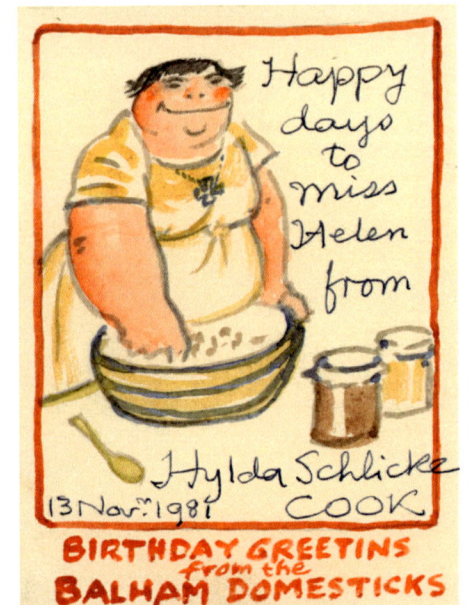

Happy days to miss Helen from
Hylda Schlicke COOK
13 Nov.ʳ 1981
BIRTHDAY GREETINS from the BALHAM DOMESTICKS

What's that terrible moaning?

I'll deal with it.

Oh! A draught.

Watching bulbs grow

Playing

We did play cards with friends, usually a game called Concentration, which only those who played with us knew. We all had our own boxes of halfpennies which were brought out at the beginning of the game.

When we lived in London, Lizie and I swam in the Tooting Bec Lido. David often came and watched.

I told you they were TOO BIG, didn't I?

48

"Disgustingly Pink!" We were there all day; but I spent most of the time in the shade – but certain people played croquet

YOU look very odd, too

We never actually used a skateboard of course, but David thought they looked tremendous fun. Why the bongo drums – who knows now?

Sisters and Family

We stayed with my Dorset sister, Anne, and family and so she got letters making arrangements and 'thank yous'. My youngest sister, Sheenagh and husband Nick, were nearer, in Bristol, and busy with babies and very young children at this time, and so we communicated by phone and just day-visits. Somehow there wasn't time there for letters. My father remarried after my mother's death, but again very few records. His birthday was February 26th, and clearly we had a family gathering for that.

30 March 88
Dearest Liz. Did I tell you that we go to
Owermoigne for Easter, to replenish
our alcohol levels and all that. We
return, all being well, on Monday.
Perhaps we can have a few LATE
eggs with you at a later date? How
about coming to GRUB on Wednesday
13th April? But come here before that
please. Love David-

THE MASTER BREWER

Anne's husband, Martin, was in the family firm, the brewers and wine merchants Eldridge Pope, while their boys Ralph and Alex were teenagers. Both my father and Anne had arthritic knees.

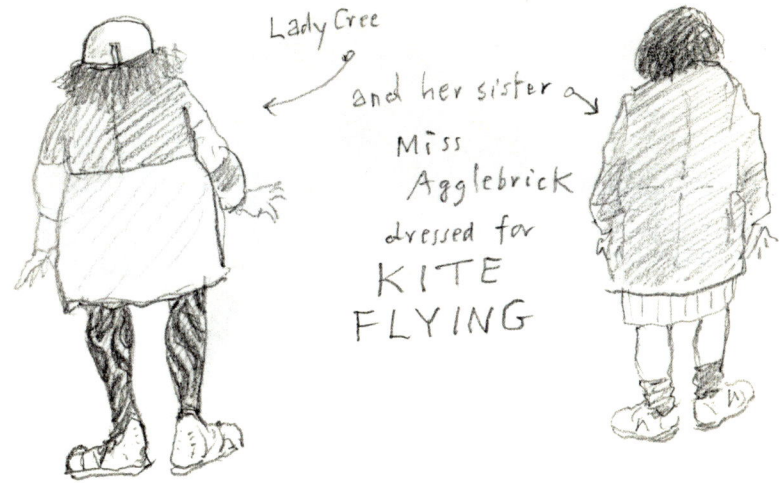

Pull your drawers hup

Lady Cree

and her sister Miss Agglebrick dressed for KITE FLYING

Kites rools OK, see

wotcher want, man?

Is this the way to Durdle Door, please

DORSET WEEKEND
8 Aug 1993

Celebrating Anne's birthday, 23 March, in her new birthday outfit. Later in life Alex became an artist, Ralph a musician.

There's an E-mail in there SOMEWHERE !!

23 March 1999

NO CONNESHUN with the Royle Cadimy

Ilex Tree wos 'ere

Me Bruffer

Me aunt

A reel cree

KEEP ON FARTIN

I come 'ome, Mum. It's cold out there and a bit creepy.

No-one turned up that I could see

map 2 1st dist.

TIT

GERRORF

COR !!

OI !

WHAZZAT ?

WOW

WOW

Pfew

A Knight in the Woods...

52

The boys had mumps when quite small.

I'm bidding....
It's.
mine.. mine..
mine

Auctioneering appeals to our Anne
Who bids up as fast as she can
For her birthday this year
She bought Weymouth Pier
In mistake for a parcel of Jam.

There were 2 boys, a pair of chump.
Who went and got themselves the m...
One, like a piglet, was covered in b....
The other came out in luminous l....

Father came in with
a touch of the g.....
Having been to the
Dentist who drew
out his s.....

XXX

And Mother said "My! How it
gives one the h....
But we musn't go down with
the deuced old d...."

The Doctor said "Ah" and then
"Hum" and then "W....!!
"I believe it's a case of South
Dussetshire Z...."

All you have to do is
read the instructions...

It didn't say
stand it on the
table

THE   PATENT TIN OPENER

Chicken Pox

Richard and Helen both worked and lived in London; Richard as a lawyer, Helen in patents. They often stayed with their three little boys – now all grown men of course – in High Croft. They were great birdwatchers. Richard got quite bad chicken pox and was off work for some time. These are some of the get-well postcards David sent. The nurse is, of course, Helen!

VISITORS

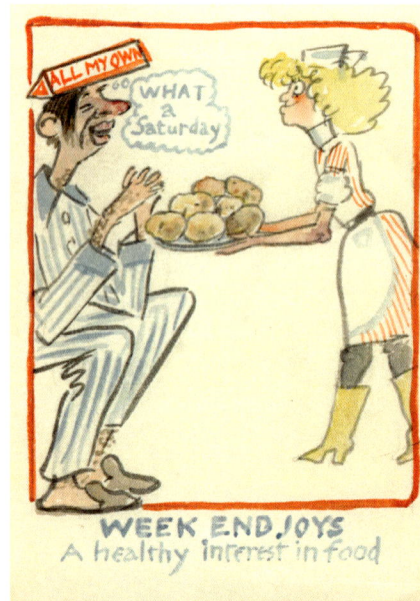

WEEK END JOYS
A healthy interest in food

THE ROAD to RECOVERY

MONDAY MORN

SUBURBAN JOYS

SUBURBAN JOYS
Entertaining visitors when convalescent.

NURSE OF THE YEAR AWARD

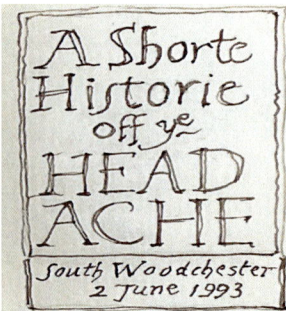

A History of the Headache

A little booklet for Eleyne Williams who suffered from bad migraines.

Headaches have been around for a long time. Primitive Man was the first to experience them as a by-product of co-inhabitation

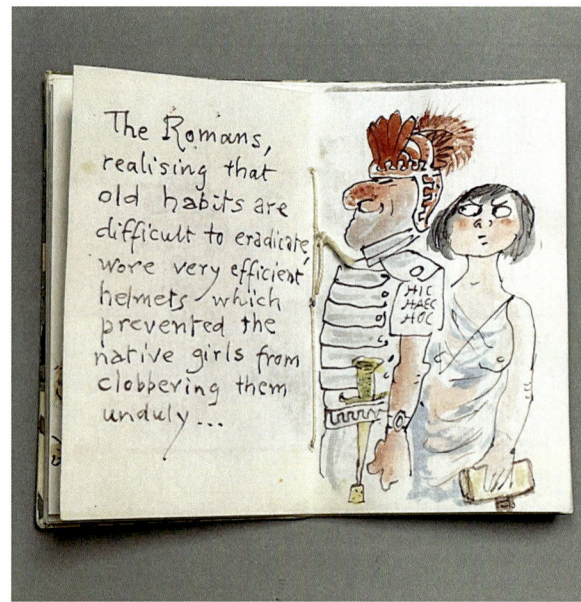

The Romans, realising that old habits are difficult to eradicate wore very efficient helmets which prevented the native girls from clobbering them unduly...

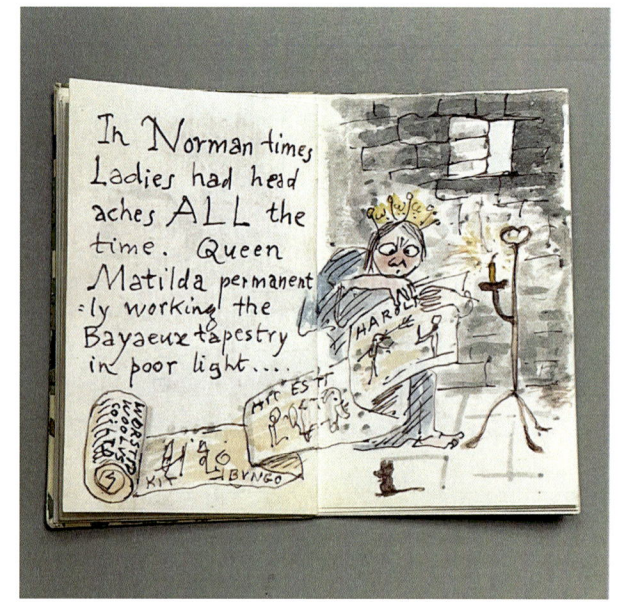

In Norman times Ladies had head aches ALL the time. Queen Matilda permanently working the Bayaeux tapestry in poor light....

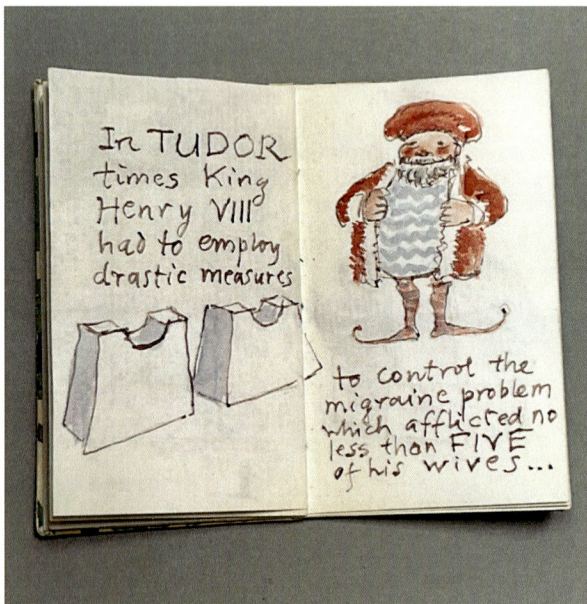

In TUDOR times King Henry VIII had to employ drastic measures to control the migraine problem which afflicted no less than FIVE of his wives...

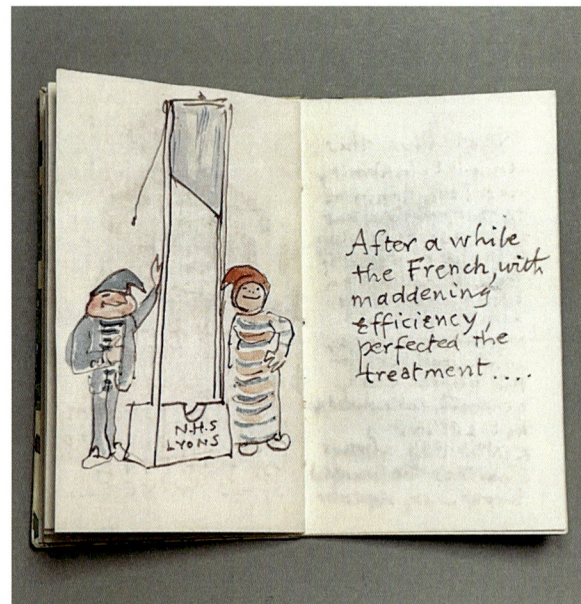

After a while the French, with maddening efficiency perfected the treatment....

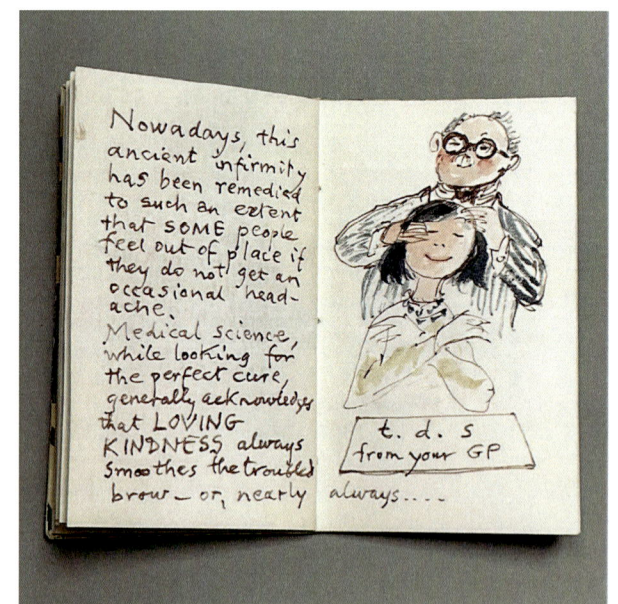

Nowadays, this ancient infirmity has been remedied to such an extent that SOME people feel out of place if they do not get an occasional head-ache.
Medical science, while looking for the perfect cure, generally acknowledges that LOVING KINDNESS always smoothes the troubled brow – or, nearly always....

Water Therapy

57

The Art of the Envelope

Many letters came in illustrated envelopes. We sometimes wondered if they became too tempting to light fingers through the postal system and so anything important went 'under brown wrapper'. Suzie Adams was Miss Palm Court Orchestra and still plays the piano at High Croft.

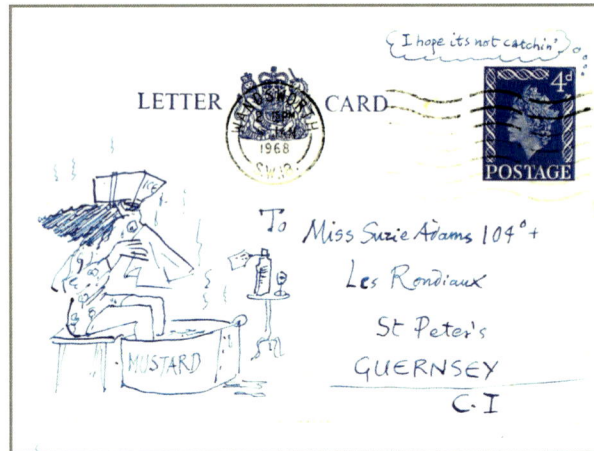

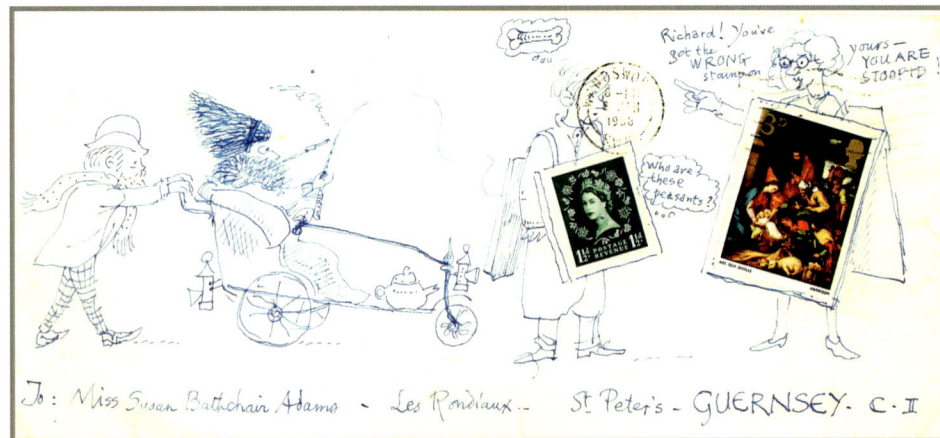

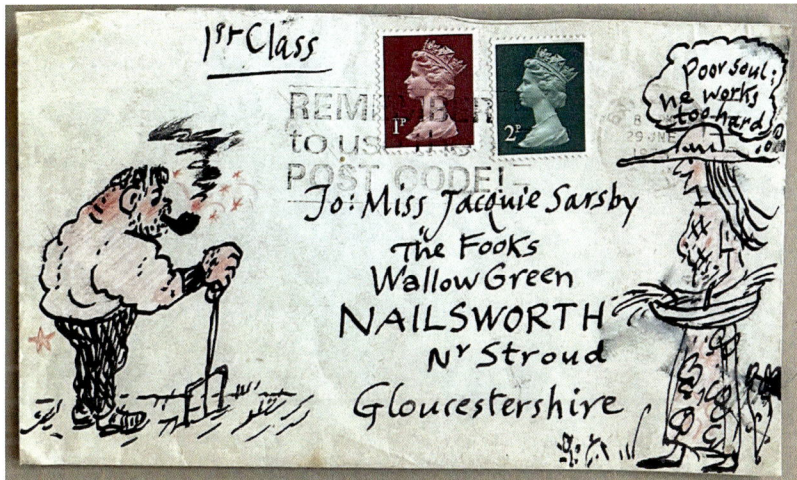

House-sitting at Mount Vernon

The two bookseller Ians went to the Antiquarian Book Fair in New York most years. They were away for a week and David house-sat in their very large, rather cold house near Stroud and looked after their cats, Henry and Bellamie.

Sunday afternoon
15 April 1979

IT'S TERRIBLE. TERRIBLE. I didn't want to go in the first place

Ooch away I dinnd pac' me pants

After running around in circles the two Ians eventually packed & set off for America, leaving

the Superannuated Hall-Porter (wearing his Gimson boots) in charge of two Diabolical Cats, who

Puddy Puddy tats

Stoopid old twit. We don't eat in the garden

were selective in their eating habits, unlike

non-pedigree mogs or alley-cats or even

Superannuated Hall-Porters who never know when to leave off.....

60

Easter Monday
16th April

Mister 'edgeping's residence

The Superannuated Man
spends his holiday in perfect
solitude at Mount Vernon

He answers the phone
- occasionally

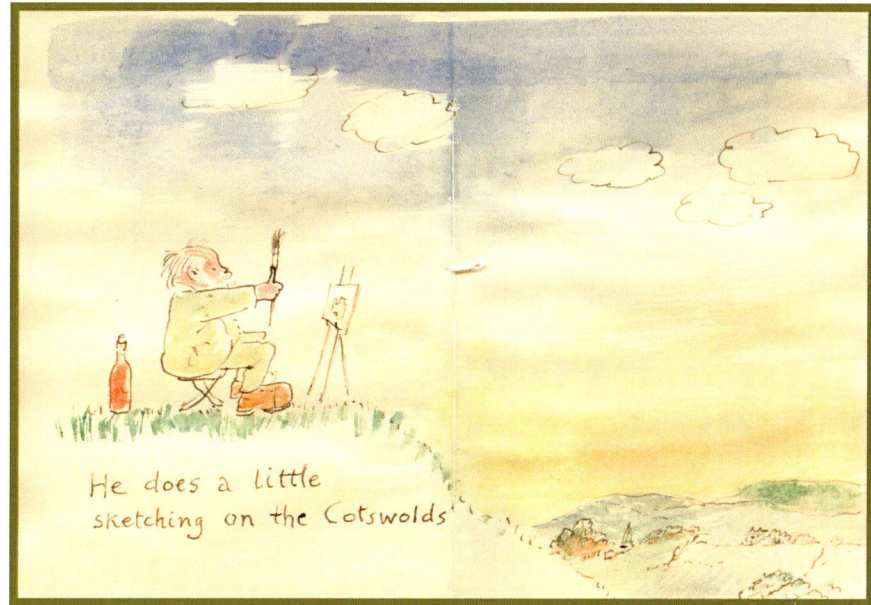

He does a little
sketching on the Cotswolds

And he sends a post
card to Dierdre who

shall I read it for you?

is in service in London
with a Mister Arnold

Tuesday 17th April
Lady Sarsby
from her Manor
at Chalford,
called; and   stroll'd   around, and

departed.

Wednesday 18th April

Begàn drawing local ruins,

follies and haunts of
ancient peace
(& all that)

Thursday 19th April

wonder if John Betjeman
has ever seen this...

Sorry 'enery, go in
yer heye did it?

A little work on gravel
paths, getting ready for

When you were in
service in Scotland
did the guests tip
you sir?

Tiresome
little man

the week-end guests to arrive and

switching off the electric blanket now that ANGEL (alias Dierdre, alias Hylda Schlicke) is coming.

Friday 20th April

The Calloways arrive...

Saturday 21st April

The General Practishener gives early morning instruction in bird song recognition to those willing to listen.

Saturday afternoon

Mount V staff caught unawares by MANDERS coming to tea

Saturday evening 21 April

Hylda Schliche's Drinks Party at Mount Vernon

Sunday 22nd April

A little gentle bird watching (requires concentration!)

Monday 23rd April St George's Day

6 am & birdsong at dawn - Hylda has to see how Dierdre is getting on....

Music and Parties

We had a few big parties and real concerts with an audience of 50-60 people in the library, but more often smaller musical evenings or dinners and then sitting around by the fire.

Highcroft, South Woodchester, Gloucestershire GL5 5EP
Telephone: 045 387 2594

Thursday 15 XI 90

Dearest Liz. It was, of course, a very special treat for us to hear the 'Goulash' Players (Hungary) and their enchanting repertoire. I hope all goes well, serpents & sackbuts & all that. O for a Tromba Marina!
Many thanks for the hospitality otherwise.
Gordon
pp Lord M

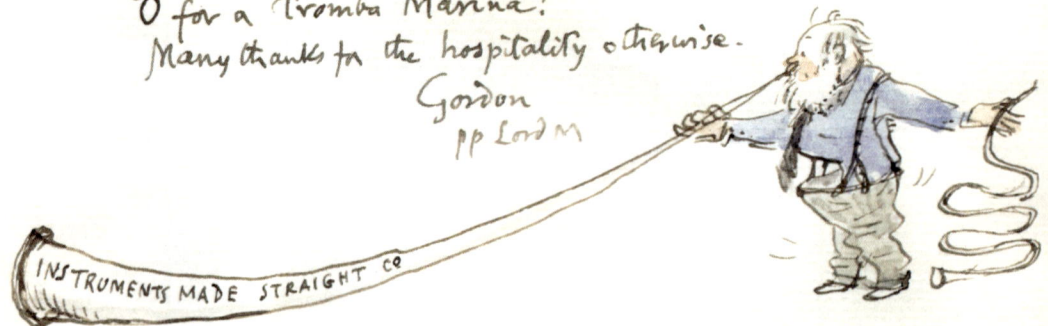

INSTRUMENTS MADE STRAIGHT Co

Laurie Lee came sometimes and forgot his scarf once. Scarves and their loss became a running joke.

the boy stood on the burning deck...

Fleurs du Mal

2·I·99

The night is made for loving and the day returns too soon, so we'll go no more a-rovin' by the light of the moon !

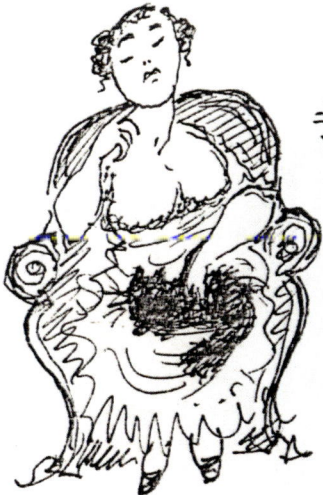

Thanksh for invitinus to your drinksh

Saturday **16** July **1994** Angel & David invite you

RSVP

HIGH CROFT South Woodchester **7.30** pm

The Ariel Wind Quintet

and Piano

Any resemblance to any persons living is purely co-incidental. This applies to the instruments as well!

Apples be ripe And nuts be brown, Petticoats up And trowsis down

Each year I sing higher and higher DETERMINED to stay in the BACH choir

66

SUNDAY
1ST JUNE
NOON - TEA
DRINKS AND
BUFFET LUNCHEON
to
CELEBRATE
ANGEL'S
BIRTHDAY
2 June 1947

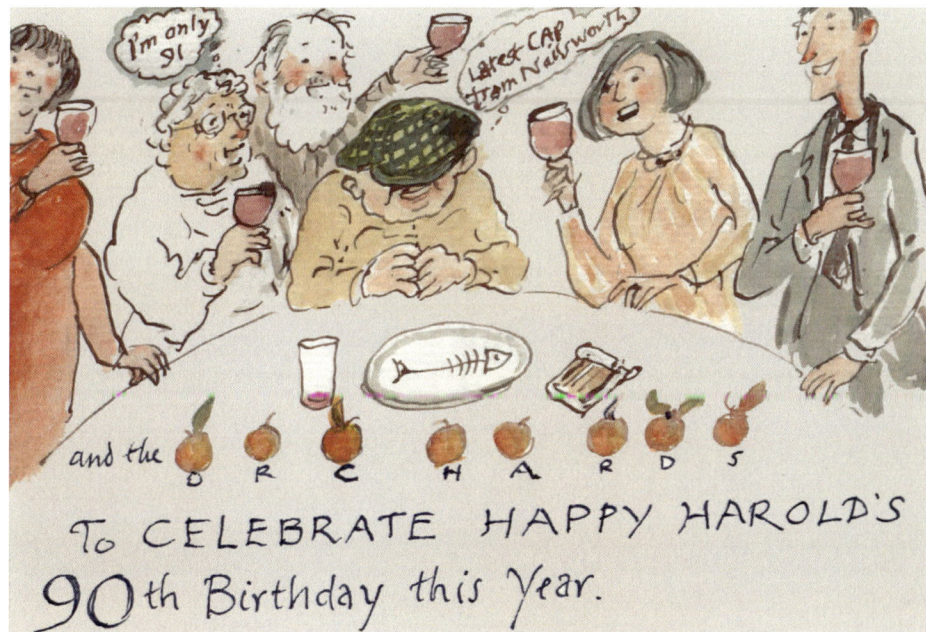

Not in our set, surely?

I always thought she was MUCH older.

So did I.

No!

In the end she did get married, I believe, to some old buffer, con--sid-er-ably (sotto voce) younger, ah hem...

HALLOWEEN
31 OCTOBER 1998

I'm only 91

Latest CAP from Nashworth

and the O R C H A R D S

TO CELEBRATE HAPPY HAROLD'S
90th Birthday this Year.

The Falconers

Toby is an architect, Ursula an artist and gilder. Ursula spent some months in Venice on a scholarship, so provided a wonderful opportunity for David to send illustrated letters. When she was there Venice was suffering from 'the big stink'. They also played croquet – hence perhaps the jolly hockey sticks of Putney High.

Monday 4th June 90

RIALTO NEWS

Highcroft, South Woodchester, Gloucestershire GL5 5EP
Telephone: 045 387 2594

oh what a terribly
hazardous experiment —
I must 'phone Venice
AT ONCE

BJC STINKS

5th July 90

Highcroft, South Woodchester, Gloucestershire GL5 5EP
Telephone: 045 387 2594

HMS TOBY

dolci canditi

Lido scuola

Determined visitor to the Lido

Tuesday 15th May '90

Caro zuccherino! At last
AT LONG LAST — a postcard
from you: and it took only
4 days to get here, post ma
10 May. This'll have to
by air-mail — 14 days is T

His Lordship graced us with his presence on Saturday last,
took food (and plenty o' gin) and regaled us with 'ALL'
gossip. I don't think the MONASTIC quarters on S. Servo
would have thrilled us: will you survive it? I hear the
you have taken a vow of silence (ahem!) and Dame Blaxill
moved... Toby's main news was that he was rushing a
over Gloucestershire looking for a future abode where you w
be accommodated in the manner to which you are accustom
..isn't sure if an ornate villa ENTIRELY cover like a cross between Mil

69

Toby and Ursula bought their house at auction, just before the arrival of the first of their three children. It was nerve-racking.

The speach bubble reads: 'So would you believe it, I put in a couple of RSJs and a pair of formula irons and they were falling all over themselves'.

Note Ursula's hats!

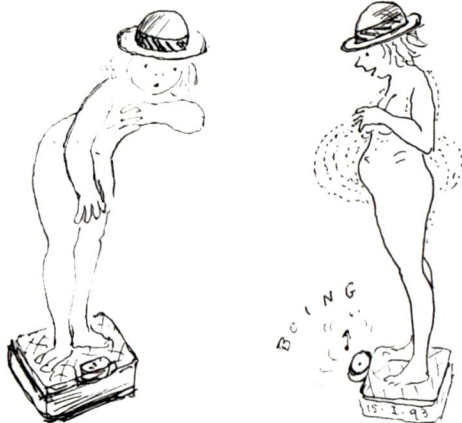

The Browns

We saw a lot and Ralph (RA) and his wife Caroline. Suppers, drinks – lots of them – and lots of funny drawings exchanged between Ralph and David. They were inveterate smokers, often trying to give up, had two little dogs, Siamese cats and for a while alpacas.

One evening game was creating new names which had to captivate the character of the person. David became Dodgi Duval, I was Dame Anne Jockelberg, Caroline, Corinna Warbler and Ralph, R. Flabworn. Ralph called David Dodgi ever after.

It said Four for the price of one, so I couldn't resist 'em

that's the VERY last straw.... I'm off....

ERE CARRIE - GEMME OUTER THIS!

EMINENT R·A EXPLOITS THE
ADVERTISING POSSIBILITIES FOR
EXTENDING THE DISTRIBUTION
OF HIS WARES, MAKES FORTUNE
AND RETIRES TO LEEDS.

For Caroline, friend of friends, with love from Angel & David, Christmas 1991 ————

EMINENT R·A DECIDES TO WORK
FROM RUBENESQUE RATHER THAN
ANOREXIC MODELS THIS YEAR

We are tewibbly solly Mister
Brawn but my colleagues and
I werry much regret we can't
shew your ordinwerry werk in OUR
gallerwee
for
wee are
TWADITIONAL

Dearest Urs, Friday 20th September 1991
I'm afraid things have gone from bad to worse with
the poor old Browns— WE ARE SO GLAD TO BE=
DIDN'T COME TO THE LECTURE AT
the Strand Sub= scription Rooms last
night. Caroline and Ralph came, got a
but bored at the end and nipped out early,
(to go to High Croft) and
to avoid being asked

if a party from the Stroud Civic Society might visit their house—
By the time me and Ange emerged into the twilight we found,
to our intense amazement, and embarrassment, that the wicked
couple had bought liquid refreshment from the 'Off licence across
the road and they were imbibing MERRILY on one of the
seats outside the Subscription Rooms!!! AND they were
being carefully monitored by TWO POLICEMEN. Quick as
a flash Ralph popped his beer bottle into Ange's bag and said
" Lesh skarp'r "....

Freud's pension recipient Resting 'one of
90 drawings which will not be shown at the Dulwich Gallery

DODGI DUVAL
GENERAL DEALER
Yamaha Catering Co
Mundy 18f July 94

Dere Mr Brown, Sir, We just got
a supply off Artistes barfs and
have reserfed you a nise one

Perhaps yewd like to corl and
see it at yore convenience.
Yores trully Dodg
P.S. Moddils extra. All sizes and
shapes in stock, guaranteed.

Looking Good

Thank goodness we rarely see ourselves as others see us.

exercise is good for the heart

I'm just going into Cotswold Woollens for 5 minutes

Ah! A little black skirt. Just what I wanted — Nice and straight.

Makes me look MUCH taller

oh no! makes me look a bit shorter....

Doesn't seem too straight!

Look the other way dear. Things weren't like this in the old days...

My gal's a Yorkshire gal, Eh bah gum she's a champion!

29.XI.94

Dearest Mary
We went to Filkins last Thursday to collect some newly rush-seated chairs.

Oooo

Ahhh

GRRR

Nearby is the Cotswold Woolen Weavers; each time we go there Angel THINKS she might buy a tweedy countrified TWO PIECE SUIT.

SALE

ROWLAND

ROWLAND'S of BATH

ROWLAND'S of BATH

How about the "extras"? WOW WOW WOW

WHAT AN ANGEL AND a Bluestocking

77

Reading to the Kitchen Maids

Tuesday 18 Nov '86

Servant's Hall
Criffel Lodge
9 Criffel Avenue
Streatham Hill
SW2

Tracey : "Cor! You don't arf read them 'arrowin' stories fit to bust me 'eart: go on wiv' this weeks episode!"

Wayne : "Lady Sarsby gazed into 'is steel blue heyes. 'Ow can I live wi'thout 'im? she thort, 'and her bosom 'eaved hup an' darn, hup an' darn, 'er corsets creakin' 'armoniously. Will 'e hever know 'ow mutch I love 'im? she sighed, Will 'e hever know the passion wivin my breast?

Tracey : Ain't that simply lovely, ain't it ....

Servant's Hall
Criffel Lodge
21st Nov '186

Tracey : Oh Mr Hodgepings, you do read so lovely. Please go on

Mr H : Lady Sarsby gazed at the moon, her teeth chattering in the cold night air, fresh from the Devon coast. She felt a strong arm on her shoulder. "Dear Heart," she murmured, slowly turning, "How can I exist without you." Imagine her horror when she turned and saw

Tracey: Fair tugs me 'eart strings, don't it Boots!

Boots: Aye, lassie, but there's mair te come: lissen a this now: Lady Sarsby couldn' contain hersen no longer. She turned to the Laird an' gazed into his steel blue heyes. "Why mock me any longer?" she implor'd him, "I've follow'd ye across the Glen & I'll no return now without an answer one way or t'other. What's it to be?" The Laird mounted his milk white steed & rode orf into the mist. Behind a rock something stirr'd....

DEIRDRE: Oh Sir, you do read so poetic. That bit about the flowers tucked behind the knocker is lovely: is it true, Sir, is it true?

ODD JOB MAN: TRUE?!! Of course it is true. Every word of it is true. Lissen a this: Lady Sarsby stood in the porch wiv' 'er 'and on 'er 'eart. Ho my Gawd, she exclaimed, would that I didn't miss 'im so mutch. Simple soul that I am, why didn't I notice the warning signs heartier. Alas alas I ham arlmost undun.... [To be cont'd in chap 4]

Staff Quarters

Criffel Castle

S.ʳ Reatham

24 Nov '86

Criffel Av: Pickle Factory

P R I Z E   1880 Recipe   O N I O N S

Lord Molesworth's Non pareil

Sob

Back to work straight away that was the LAST chapter

LORD & MASTER :   This is pre-posterous! Pull yourself together girl!! That d*****d Butler has been reading too many lurid stories to you. Goodness knows what goes on below stairs nowadays: time was when we made sure there weren't any penny dreadfulls around; but can't stem the tide to-day. And what absolute rubbish — ALWAYS ends in tears and tantrums, does it? Bah! Humbug! Things weren't like this in the old days. Come, come, stop that d*****d sniffling and snivelling. Why are you crying so much?

DIERDRE :   It's 'ercule, sirrh, 'e keeps making pickled onions...

"Excuse me, Sirroh, bud we hash^t 'ad chapters 7 and 8 of dat werry Romantick Mellowdramah, has we?"

At Breakfast   Saturday 22nd

This is my un-birthday drawing to you with much love from all the staff at Criffel Castle.

Lord Molesworth says he doesn't feel he is a day younger than 70 now that he has his Senior Citizen's Pass —

Much love as ever from
Arye n' Dave

Fun with Friends

Sylvia delivered our milk every day, and straw for our strawberry bed. She visited relatives in Australia one year. Another Australian connection was through Lizie (second name Suzie) who thought, briefly of a job there and then left her shoes behind.

Eric de Maré was, in his day, a famous photographer. We only met him as an old man and what I shall always remember him for is his saying, in quite a pronouced Swedish accent, 'I don't understand the young, their MANIA for work and GETTING ON. Why don't they just ENJOY LIFE? Forget this MANIA.'

OLD FASHIONED CAMERAS ARE BEST !

Confrontation with William Morris and EBJ.

COTSWOLD CAVALCADE
-------- ---------

A New Album of slightly-faded Sepia Photographs

by

KIT WILLIAMS
--- --------

To be published 1st January 1991 as follows:

Strictly limited edition of 20 De luxe copies bound in full calf limp with shrimp and nicotine staining, lettered in avenue gold.   £250.-

If called for at a later date an unlimited edition in paperback, for inclusion in cornflake packets.

APPLY TO: Rolph Prawn, Publisher, Ambly, Glos., or to the above.

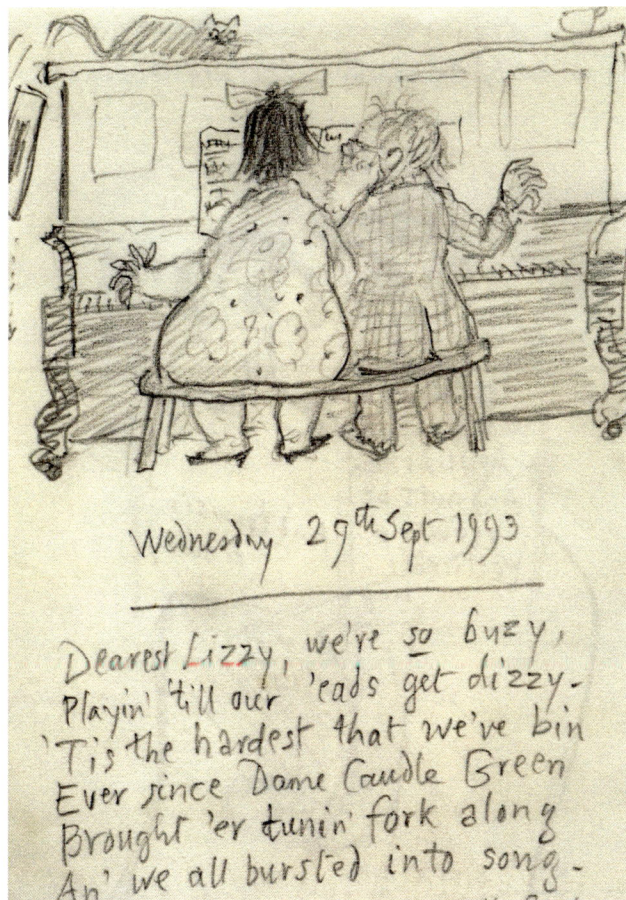

Wednesday 29th Sept 1993

Dearest Lizzy, we're so buzy,
Playin' 'till our 'eads get dizzy.
'Tis the hardest that we've bin
Ever since Dame Candle Green
Brought 'er tunin' fork along
An' we all bursted into song.

The Milkado

Apropos . . .
nothing in particular

When we were in London, David had a gallery with Christopher Hewett, Taranman, for a short while. Here they are hanging an exhibition. I had a little motorbike, complete with suitable protective clothing. I just couldn't leave these out.

THESE ARE FATTENING NIBBLES

NICE SQUARE BICCIES

Dave - you aint changed your socks . . .

"A fairly recent example I think."

Lord Molesworth's
last appearance at
Glyndebourne. Needless
to say he rarely looked like
this!

So Who was David Gould?

humourist

grump

money-man

handiman

bookworm

caricaturist

painter

printer

crossword whizz

poet

bonviveur

expert

boyscout

musician

doctor

rambler

aristocrat

He was a man of many parts.

Acknowledgements

I met Jane Dorner in 2022 and we talked about how I had begun this book, but then was beaten by my lack of computer skills. Jane said she would help me and we started work. Without her these pictures would have remained locked in my computer and been largely unseen. Each one went through mysterious enhancement processes in Photoshop which involved removing folds in the paper (not always possible), coffee stains, writing that detracted from the images, some letterheading, the odd bit of foxing and much more. Jane was also able to do the layout in InDesign and we spent several months collaborating; she was very patient with all the times I changed my mind. I am very, very grateful to her not only for all the computing knowledge and input but also for the fun she brought to creating the book.

My thanks to Sanderson Design Group for allowing me to use the Willow Boughs William Morris wallpaper, that we have always had in our houses, for the endpapers of this book. David often used it to cover his little booklets.

My lasting thanks must, of course, go to all the friends who lent me their letters and little notes from David to scan or photograph. Without them where would the fun have been?